OLD GROWTH FOREST

To Ann & David
with love
Grace

OLD GROWTH FOREST

BY

GRACE HAWES

www.bookstandpublishing.com

Published by
Bookstand Publishing
Morgan Hill, CA 95037
3913_3

ISBN 978-1-61863-538-9

Printed in the United States of America

"Every language is an
old-growth forest
of the mind…"

Wade Davis

Dedicated to my

dear friends

in

our corner of

the

Herbert Hoover Memorial Building

TABLE OF CONTENTS

CHARLOTTE"S WEB

When I sat with

    my young children

    weeping over the death

        of a fictional spider

I was reminded once again

      of the power

       of a

        few simple words

CAUTION

A good way to

    induce sleep

    is to imagine yourself

    lying in the sand on a

warm beach

        while friendly

        little waves

        rhythmically

        caress your feet

        and dragonfly wings

            gently brush

            your sun-warmed cheeks

If you're not asleep by now however

    watch out

    for everything changes

        the warm sand itches

the insects bite

the heat

    suffocates

and the waves

    toss ashore

    slimy

    stinging

    jellyfish

Always

    use fantasy with care

BRITISH CARS ARE LIKE THAT

After twenty years of marriage

he bought a classic

bright red MG

    (cheaper and safer than a girlfriend)

        but a poor choice

It could *not*

    be faithful

    and always

    spent more time

        with mechanics

           than it did

           with him

HAIKU

Being a fellow

apple-lover I know why

Eve couldn't resist

BOOBY TRAP

The ceramic teapot

has a tiny dragon's head

peeping out of the lid

    for good luck

Unfortunately

    hot water

        causes

        the unglazed interior

        to emit

          lethal fumes

            that even the lucky

            dragon

              can't destroy

A FEW NOTES

Music's indelible imprint

    coded to record

      the past

   returns unbidden and

     a few notes

        unheard for years

    elicit

    instant replay

DECEMBER 22

Two people

      very close to me

      died in different years

      on the same day

A coincidence so cruel

      that every year since

            the solstice steals the

            light

            and memories

            steal the

            season

EDUCABLE

Years ago

in a man's world

women were

out of place in

> hardware stores
> lumber yards
> auto shops
> > etcetera

but only one time

do I remember us

> egregiously showing
> our ignorance

My friend needed tires

> I went with her

"Four tires, please,"
> she requested
> at the counter

"What size do you wish to purchase, madam?"
> the imperious
> clerk inquired

"Aren't they," she asked
        mildly surprised
        and a bit confused
                since surely he must
                know this,
                        "ONE SIZE FITS ALL?"

Of course
        he did know and
        managed
        not to guffaw

In the years since

        we've learned and learned

        steadily crossing old barriers

                intimidated no longer
                by
                hardware stores
                lumber yards

        or auto shops
                where we now

                        confidently
                                ask for tires
                                in their
                                appropriate sizes

TOLL

In the

    Chinese cloisonné factory

  we marveled

      at the

      exquisite

      intricacy

      of every object

Later

  we learned

      many workers

      die of

      lead poisoning

The detailed beauty of

  each piece of art

  takes

      its pound of flesh

DISPLACED

They came from many places

    with

        Old World antagonisms

        that

        in America

        they suppressed

            while the shards remained in

            their

             papers

            and their

            bittersweet memories

HAIKU

Ospreys are black and

white – tuxedoed Fred Astaires

of the wild bird world

WANDERLUST SATIATED

To travel many times

in

many places

liberates you

when

roadblocks

overshadow the

path ahead

UNFORGETTABLE

In a new location

every year

    summer vacations

    were to be

    fun and

        educational

        according to the parents

The kids

    unaware of the ulterior motive

        learned from both

        enjoyment

        and ambience

            since they arrived together

            hand in hand

BARGAIN

There's a small brightly colored

jar on the kitchen shelf

a little treasure that

Marianne and I

found at Harrod's

the place to go in London

if you want to buy gold bars

a $5000 handbag

an $800 collar for your dog

Or to ferret out

a perfect little memento

like we did

It says"Jam" on one side

and "Confiture" on the other

Bilingual and cheap

What more could you ask?

PATRIOTISM

We were so imbued

    with love of

    country in grade school

    that to this day

    when we sing the

        national anthem

           at a ball game

    my eyes

    fill with tears

HARVEST

Grapes come in clusters

    poems do too

One needs a season to ripen

    the other a lifetime

EXTINCT VOLCANOS

We'd like to think

    we rattled the earth

    and spewed forth

        molten heat

        in our youth

DREAM ON

Very slowly

    I make my way
        past the shoe department

        flats
        ballet slippers
        Nikes
            popular fashion
                no temptation
Then I get to
        very very very
            high heels that sparkle
I'll just try them on
        I say

They fit beautifully
        and don't hurt *that* much

I totter to the mirror
        and grin

I'm so tall
        so slender
            so *youthful*

I totter back to sit down

No I say to the salesman
        but thanks for the memory

POETIC LICENSE

Some people

mistakenly believe that

all poetry and prose are

entirely *autobiographical*

unaware that

imagination

is the flint

and the fire

A MODERN FAIRY TALE

Once upon a time
    for many years
    in the middle of the 20th century
    Progress and Good Times prevailed

For a young
    couple
    with small children

    California
    was an ever-upward
           exciting
           success story
      new homes
      new neighborhoods
      new friends
      new schools

    all of it amidst
      the reliable sunshine
      of year-round
        good weather
The young couple were
    married in a
    formal ceremony
      arranged
      and cheerfully paid for
      by their approving parents
      who besides footing the bill
      gave them a sturdy
      Detroit-built sedan

They worked hard
joined a country club
partied with friends
all the while
assured that
their children
(wearing braces
on their carefully
brushed and
flossed teeth)
were thriving
in secure
serene
Leave-It-To-Beaver lives

The hard-working couple prospered steadily
always saving money for
the children's college

always confident that their offspring
were on the right path
following Mom and Dad in their
steadfast footsteps

But my oh my

you *know* what happened

A Generation Gap of monstrous proportions

opened before them

a chasm of opposing expectations

Instead of cut-outs of themselves they'd expected
        the couple
                hatched

        BOOMERS

        a whole new overpowering
        demographic
        who had the temerity
                to say
                        we don't trust
                        anyone over 30

        who wouldn't fight in
                Uncle Sam's army
        who smoked strange stuff
        who relied on the pill
        who refused to get steady jobs
        who wanted to "live off the land"
        who quit going to church and
                believed in a Maharishi

    TURN ON
    TUNE IN
    DROP OUT
        the kids chanted

The couple
        bewildered and distraught at first
        eventually recovered
                they *were* resourceful as you've
                probably figured out by now
        and said

OK kids, have it your way

They sold the family home they'd
    bought for $25,000
        for a million-plus
    invested the handsome profit wisely
        bought a luxurious motorhome

        and left town

When their not-so-young-any-longer kids
    protested

            Wait a minute
                they said
            We're planning to move back in

The couple replied

        Gosh we're sorry
            but you should know by now

            the times they are a-changin'

and so

        wintering in Miami
        summering in Maine

        they lived

            happily ever after

GRISAILLE

A lovely French word

   meaning a style of

monochromatic

   painting

   in shades of gray

      perfect for artists in Paris

      and

      coincidentally in

      Shanghai
      London and
      Portland too

FIGHT! FIGHT!

The cry went up on the

playground

and we all ran to watch

   one kid beat up another

We were on our own

   at recess

and whatever animal

instincts we indulged in

went unnoticed

and unreported

   (back in the day)

EARLY BIRD

The sun makes long shadows

    across the quiet campus

The air is still and cool

I take deep breaths

    as I cross

        the empty parking lot

           toward the building

               where I work

I walk slowly

    because I love every minute of

    this glorious time of day

As I get closer I look up

    to the top of

    the tower Herbert Hoover built

        its shadow

at this hour

longer than its height

My building is next door

but I always look up once more (old habit)

before going inside

I meet no one as

I make my way

on the stairs and

down the long hallway to

the door with my name

I open it

turn on the light and

reach in the drawer for a tea bag

and my cup

then down the hall a few

more steps for hot water

At my desk
    the room now filled
    with the scent of herb tea

I turn on the computer

    search for my to-do list

    and begin my workday

      knowing that

      tomorrow

      I will again bask in the

      early morning

      illusion

      of having the

        Stanford University

        campus

          all to myself

HAIKU

Eccentricity

Is a trait that endears or

Drives others crazy

SPECTRE

We scared ourselves silly

   for most of the

   twentieth century

   with a rabid fear of

   Communist countries

       controlled
          not by
          Marx's
          classless
          stateless
          moneyless
              social order
      but by
      ruthless dictators

Of course

   we were probably right

      to be scared of them

PUBLIC WORKS

There were six men

in hard hats

      with their hands in their

        pockets

      staring down a hole in the street

        this morning

They must have

    decided something

      because this afternoon

      six other men

        with shovels

      are making the hole

        much

        deeper

CALIFORNIA PIONEER

Alice Park lived from

1861 to 1961

a person of little consequence

in the larger scheme of things

but Alice

had the strength of her

convictions

Very early in the

20th century

she was a pacifist
socialist
vegetarian
feminist
long before her beliefs

became

an intrinsic part

of California's ethos

(Alice Park is one of my favorite "paper" friends.)

ROOM SERVICE, PLEASE

The bed with the thick coverlet

    in Lucerne

the deep old-fashioned bathtub

    in London

the view from Chateau Lake Louise

    in Banff

the wake-up call of the muezzin

    in Kashgar

the chocolates on the pillow

    in Carmel

the iron balcony overlooking the Seine

    in Paris

Put them all together

    and move in

        forever

AH YOUTH

When we were young

    the lyrics of

    September Song

    haunted our imagination

        with the

        romantic urgency

            of dwindling days

Ah youth

FLORAL IED

New surroundings

    bring

all kinds

of surprises

    like the time

    I picked armloads

    of poison oak to

        decorate our home

        with

        fall color

WORDS

When she was

       in her eighties

      and I wasn't

she told me

      the saddest part

         of growing old is

            losing your

            vocabulary

WORRY

Like the wind before

a storm

foretelling its

onset

the unease of my

midnight mind

precedes

the dread

of the

day to come

INQUIRY

The room was full of

    old friends

        some alive
        some dead

She wasn't sure which he was

    until he came close

        and said

            Why did you leave

            without

            telling me

Do you have to know *now*

    she thought

and wished he'd

get out of her dream

INFO

Falling in love

      at first sight

      doesn't reveal

      all you need to know

Falling in lust

      at first sight

      does

DROUGHT

The only memory we have

    of that summer

    is the grasshoppers

        scratching our bare legs

           as they jumped on us

                from all directions

           hoping for relief

                finding none

MY FIRST PET

He was a stray

who made his living

hanging around a

crab factory

eating whatever

anyone tossed him

soon smelling like

tainted seafood

and laughingly called

Fragrance

We adopted him

bathed away the awful odor

and eliminated forever

his only drawback

DISTANCE MATTERED

Our high school band uniforms

    were made of wool

    appropriately

    comfortably warm

       for most of the year

          up North

             but sweat lodges of

             scratching misery

             in a 90-degree heat wave

Only our youth

    and the short
    three-block
    small town
    Main Street
    parade routes
        saved us from
        melting in a jumble of
        metal horns and
        red wool

THE GIFT

of damask napkins

family heirlooms

imbued with

an acrimonious heritage of

disappointment and

disapproval

were

for the next generation merely

deftly patterned

squares of cloth

unblemished by

stains of use

or shards of animus

'TIS THE SEASON

The hundred-foot pine

    across the way

grows in a

      jagged uneven pattern

        until the very top

        where it tapers

          into a perfect

          Christmas tree

            decorated

            with

            glistening tinsel of

              ice

              and snow

TOO CLOSE FOR COMFORT

We walked on

    the train tracks

    for miles

        listening for the

        4:15 to St. Paul

One day we

    stood by

    and watched it

    flatten our pennies

We never went back

Hearing the whistle at 4:15

    was

    as close as we

    cared to be

LITTLE WOMEN

Every Sunday morning

the neighbors

watched them go by

    five beautiful sisters on their

    way to church

        all in white dresses

            with tiny hand-stitched smocking

                on each bodice

        their lace-edged skirts

            just touching the top of

                soft leather shoes

        their long dark red hair

            tied back

            with white ribbons

It was like watching

the March sisters plus one

smiling and beautiful

always together

always harmonious

Only on closer inspection

could the neighbors

have seen the difference

for unlike

Meg and Jo and Beth and Amy

these sisters did not like

one another

and lived daily off of the

psychic nourishment

each received from criticizing

the others

Sad to say

the bitter young ladies

never married

lived together forever

in the family home

and became

not surprisingly

bitter old maids

Yet always

the neighbors stared

with pleasure

at the lovely sight

of them

walking to church

on Sunday morning

SCAREDY CATS

She lived alone

    in a small

    rundown house

        set far back

        from the street

She was old and frail

    tiny and bent

        harmless as a moth

    but we ran and ran for our lives

    when we saw her

Old Lady Melby is a witch

    the big kids told us

She turns little squirts

    like you

    into

toads

they said

So we ran and ran

escaping *danger*

our imaginations

wild with the fear

of living life in a

swamp

WANING

The world's a lonelier

place as time

goes on

and losses exceed

gains

ASK THE NRA

Does the

       right to bear arms

       mean

       we'll soon carry

              small

              individual

              nuclear

              devices

       to go safely to the

              grocery store

              in case a

              Redskin or a

              Redcoat

                     leaps out at us?

EXODUS

Every summer

    the chipmunks came back

They lived under

    the cottage all season

      and were the

      best of neighbors

Then one year

    for no known reason

they disappeared

    never to return

Nothing ever changed at the cottage

    until the year

    the chipmunks left

I THINK I CAN

How wonderful it was

    the other day

    to read that

    milk chocolate

        is as good for you as dark

The only catch is

    it takes *more* of it

    for the

    same results

What a sacrifice

But doable

NOVEMBER 23, 1963

Nothing of consequence

happened to us today

Like most days in our lives

nothing unusual happened

It was cloudy and windy

we spent the afternoon

picking up walnuts

that fell on the ground

all week

It was an ordinary day

And oh, we are going to need

many many

ordinary days

like today

for a long long time

to come

FEAST OR FAMINE

Being out of sorts

is often due to too much

to eat or too little

SUNDAY AFTERNOON

At one grandma's

    there are lots of cousins to see

at the other's

    none

        just the two of us

        expected to be

            good little girls

            for what seems like

            an eternity of

                dragging hours

                looking at

                stereopticon pictures

                we've already seen

                two

                    million

                        times

TOP SECRET

Many years ago

    my daughter

        tucked a folded note

        behind the

        baseboard

        in her closet

We sold the house

    a short while later

        and the message

        lingers on

           unread

                by posterity

            undisclosed by the

                author

TALENT

How wonderful

    it must be

    to open

    your mouth and have

        an aria

        float into the air

MAYBE THEY'RE NOT GOING TO STAY

Small town audiences

    arrive the very

    last minute at

    public events

        assured that

        there'll always be

            a parking space and

            an empty seat

They do this in Portland too

    as if

        denial

            will send

            a couple million

            back where they

                came from

ROAD JOCKEY

In Mexico City

      he darted in and out
        skidding
        screeching
        leaning on the horn
            competing for fares

When we hired him to

      take the two of us on a

      leisurely trip

        in the mountains

    his big city

        driving skills came too

That we survived

      a long wild weekend

        with him at the wheel

    is still one of life's

      mysteries

PREPARATION?

Sometimes I wonder

    if anyone in Washington

    read

    Afghan history

       before

          we

          got into

             our

             longest war

FRIENDSHIP DIMISHED

Richard loved animals

    every living thing

    no matter how humble or profuse

    so when my son

    jovially poked

    one of his caterpillars

he came to our door

    trembling with righteous indignation

    to report to me

I inquired after his "pet" (it was fine)

    and assured him that

    his best friend would

    come to apologize soon

OK he said

but tell John

I don't like him

as much as I used to

EMPIRE

It's a big responsibility

    being the world's keeper

Others

    though envious

    will criticize

And a thousand years later

    history's judgment

    may very well

      be

    unkind

ALL JUST GET ALONG? NOT LIKELY

An item on the back pages
    of the paper
        the other day
    caught my eye

It seems the Prime Minister of a
    small country

        celebrating its
        100th anniversary
            of independence
            from the
            Ottoman Empire
                (with a huge parade
                and an 18-ton cake)

    referred in a speech to his nation's
        former
            more extensive
        boundaries
    thereby
    angering
    all the neighbors
        who assumed it was
        a resurgence
            of belligerent acquisitive
                aspirations
    and at once cancelled
    their plans
        to join the
        celebration

Tempest in a teapot? Yes

And also
 another
 present-day
 reminder
 of how close to the surface
  and ubiquitous
 are ancient
  unforgiving
   animosities

GONE BUT NOT FORGOTTEN

The past

The past

The past

We drag it along

    like a duffel bag

    full of boulders

VIRGINIA WOOLF WOULD APPROVE

It was the only

part of the house

    I had never seen

        until one time

        when we ventured there

        together

My dad went up the ladder first

    I was next

        all excited

    then my mother

At the top my dad

    pushed open the

    mysterious little door

    pulled on a long string

        and the lone bulb

        hanging from the ceiling

illuminated a big empty space

empty except for

small boxes

in one corner

that my parents

rifled through

I walked around

ever so slowly

contemplating

calculating

imagining

a *secret* room

a refuge from all the cares

of the 3rd grade

The fact that the ladder

to get there

had to be in the middle

of the dining room

to reach the trapdoor

and the fact that

my parents would never

let me climb the ladder

alone

did nothing to

squelch my

wildly blossoming

fantasy

A room of my own

OLD GROWTH

Layers of experience

enhance the original

    with a patina of

    seasoned

    knowing

WAAAAAY OFF BROADWAY

All summer long

    in Lois's garage

        we wrote plays

        made scenery

        acted all the parts

        sold tickets

        kept the cash

If the "critics" were unkind

    we didn't care

We were too busy

    entertaining

    one another

DOUBLE-EDGED SWORD

Like a river

eroding its banks

    change

        transforms

        both the

        powerful

        and the

        weak

RESPITE

Such a short path

    from the back door

    to the embracing arbor

        a tiny haven

        covered by the

            tangled shade

            of clematis vines

        furnished with

            wicker chairs

            and a table

                just big enough

                for a teacup and a muffin

Twenty steps from

    chaos to calm

A journey of a thousand miles

HISTORICAL RESEARCH

Every now and again

    in the Archives

we found letters

    with penciled postscripts

The writers expected their

    discreet messages

    to be erased

The recipients forgot

    and presented history

      with intriguing pieces

    to add

      to the puzzle

ANIMAL FARM

When an American couple

    thrilled

    at the sight of hundreds (maybe thousands)

    of pheasants

        as far as the eye could see

a fellow traveler set them straight

"You see, the birds aren't wild,
    as you thought.
  They're raised and released
    for city people
      who come to
      Yorkshire
        and pay to kill them.

  It's a shooting gallery

    with live targets."

GO FIGURE

It is amazing

> how many

> of the

> world's greatest despots

> wrote poetry

THE WAGON WHEEL SUPPER CLUB

It was in rural

    Wisconsin's

        countryside

        near the Illinois border

The food was good

      mostly red meat
      and large portions

The bar had a three-piece combo

     with a pretty singer

        (married to the bass player)

     who sang "On the Sunny Side of the Street"

        every evening

My friend and I

    were neophyte

    waitresses

who dropped out of

college

to earn next year's tuition

Our uniforms

were ankle-length dresses

and starched white aprons

in keeping no doubt

with the

Wagon Wheel motif

The Manager was the mistress

of the married owner

or so we heard

She looked a bit

like Wallis Simpson

and always seemed to be

in a bad mood

except when her hairdresser

didn't get it quite right

then she

went into a rage that

spilled over onto

anyone in sight

We soon learned to

stay as far away

as possible

which wasn't always

far enough

The other person we tried

to avoid

was the Chef

Now there was a man

who not only swore

in eloquent

imaginative

English but also in

two or three languages

we didn't understand

The Manager was Empress

of the dining room

where she greeted customers

with whatever charm she could muster

where the lighting was dim

and the only sound

the happy diners

chatting over dinner

The Chef was Emperor of the

kitchen

an underworld

of bright lights and noise

of shoving
swearing
sweating and
banging

of scurrying waitresses yelling

"Coming Through"

as they backed into the

swinging doors

balancing huge round trays

piled high with orders going out

and dirty dishes coming in

We only worked at the Wagon Wheel a

few months

not long enough for it to be
the School of Hard Knocks

but it was there we found out

how lucky we were

to be going back

to Madison

TAKE THAT

We knew nothing

about him

a small town mystery

without

family or friends

Not that we cared

all that much

We just wanted

the candy money

we received for

old newspapers

and magazines

we sold him

As fast as we could

we made the

transaction

in his dark

dingy (kind of scary) shop

and hurried away

counting our pennies

laughing

behind his back

***

Who got the last laugh?

Today

the one and only

elaborately decorated

marble mausoleum

in the entire city

cemetery

is his

A lavish memorial

paid for by the money

    he saved

        from dealing

        in other people's

        junk

BETWEEN THE LINES

Reading what was

on the page

was enough

That the author's words

needed

interpretation

never occurred to us

until

our high school

English teacher

thrust the

thought into our

simple minds

BUT HOW TO ACCESS THE EXCESS

We flew through

    a dense cloud cover

    yesterday into a

    world of dazzling

    sunshine

        every bit of it

        going to waste

            when

            down below

                oh

                how we would bask

                and frolic

WAY TO GO

She died

knowing

that

for her

there was nothing

left

undone

In a long

rich

life

she had

happily

done it all

(Inspired by the obituary of a woman I wish
I'd known)